PERICLES

ATHENIAN STATESMAN AND PATRON OF THE ARTS

Leaders of the Ancient World™

PERICLES

ATHENIAN STATESMAN AND PATRON OF THE ARTS

BEATRIZ SANTILLIAN AND
HAMISH AIRD

Rosen YA™
NEW YORK

Published in 2018 by The Rosen Publishing Group, Inc.
29 East 21st Street, New York, NY 10010

First Edition

Library of Congress Cataloging-in-Publication Data

Names: Santillian, Beatriz, author. | Aird, Hamish, co-author.
Title: Pericles : Athenian statesman and patron of the arts / Beatriz Santillian and Hamish Aird.
Description: First edition. | New York : Rosen Publishing, 2018. | Series: Leaders of the ancient world | Audience: Grades 7 to 12. | Includes bibliographical references and index.
Identifiers: LCCN 2016053654 | ISBN 9781508174875 (library bound)
Subjects: LCSH: Pericles, approximately 495 B.C.-429 B.C.—Juvenile literature. | Statesmen—Greece—Athens—Biography—Juvenile literature. | Orators—Greece—Athens—Biography—Juvenile literature. | Art patrons—Greece—Athens—Biography—Juvenile literature. | Athens (Greece)—Politics and government—Juvenile literature. | Democracy—Greece—Athens—History—To 1500—Juvenile literature.
Classification: LCC DF228.P4 S27 2018 | DDC 938/.04092 [B] —dc23
LC record available at https://lccn.loc.gov/2016053654

Manufactured in the United States of America.

On the cover: Marble bust of Pericles.

CONTENTS

INTRODUCTION 6

CHAPTER 1
THE YOUNG PERICLES 10

CHAPTER 2
THE YOUNG POLITICIAN 27

CHAPTER 3
WAR 47

CHAPTER 4
THE GOLDEN YEARS 67

CHAPTER 5
GATHERING CLOUDS 81

GLOSSARY 99
FOR MORE INFORMATION 101
FOR FURTHER READING 105
BIBLIOGRAPHY 106
INDEX 108

INTRODUCTION

In the fifth century BCE, Athens was going through structural changes that would be celebrated beyond the following two and a half millennia. The advent of democracy, resistance against the Persian Empire, and facing down waves of destruction would completely rearrange the face and function of Athens, while preserving the most basic principles, freedom and independence. At its heart, the people of Athens were always pushing for what they cared about.

Pericles (ca. 495–429 BCE) would personally witness some of these changes and would advocate for a sometimes-progressive, sometimes-militant philosophy that relied on principles of freeing his people from danger and domination. Without ever becoming king in a nation that relied on democratic rule, Pericles was a citizen in a high military position who was particularly pushy when consensual agreement wasn't enough in order to enact his reforms. But he wasn't a tyrant—there was never any Athenian blood on his hands when pushing through a political change. Instead, he engaged in spectacular political maneuvering to overcome his domestic enemies and fund construction projects

This map depicts Greece shortly before Pericles came to power. It is labeled to show how the Greeks dealt with the conflict that pitted them against the Persian Empire.

that probably weren't commonly thought of as the responsibility of a member of the military.

Our certainty of the facts of Pericles's life varies. The historians of his time, along with those who were looking back to his era, included Plutarch, Herodotus, Thucydides, and others who thought it was fit to inquire into the events of history. Regarding a certain contemporary of Pericles's, Vincent Azoulay discusses a reason to be sceptical of primary sources in his book *Pericles of Athens*: "Thucydides, himself a stratēgos, was far from being as 'objective' as a certain line of historiography has long maintained." This offers one reason that Thucydides, in particular, had a biased perspective. He wrote from the point of view of a marginal set of values: he shared the same career as Pericles, the subject of his writing. The fact that they had a personal relationship offers that much more reason to question his ability to portray the facts without a particularly positive or negative bias.

There are reasons to scrutinize sources from authors who didn't live during Pericles's time, or who didn't have a first-hand witness of the events they recorded—but there are also reasons to trust them. When measuring whether a recorded event happened, it is possible to confirm or question whether the record is accurate against another account. The same event may appear in a tomb, or a corpse or tool may show contrary proof of some claim. For example, Herodotus's works were often claimed to be credible in the sense that archaeological evidence confirmed the basics of his claims. But while events he wrote about are likely to have happened, the quantities he offers for details like the number of soldiers Xerxes I gathered during the second Persian invasion of Greece are more likely than not very inaccurate.

Being aware of these issues allows historians to be honest about both what we know and which topics need further research. While taking a creative approach that goes well beyond looking at texts, we must recognize that the artifacts we encounter serve political purposes that require a certain level of distrust. They don't record facts, so there is much that we can never be sure of.

But we do know that the Greeks were there. They fought each other, and they banded together to fight foreign enemies. They were proud people who were led by proud men, and they left us as many clues as they could about who they were.

CHAPTER 1

THE YOUNG PERICLES

As with most who would join the ruling class, Pericles grew up in the wake of privilege. These advantages, in addition to his natural and cultivated talents, led him to the top of the military chain. But even as a participant in military life, he would not be hardened to the needs of the people.

BOYHOOD

We can picture Pericles growing up in one of those plain white houses within the walls of Athens. All around there would have been a lot of building activity, first of the fortifications and then of the houses. The Persians had been very systematic in their destruction of the city in 480 BCE. Famous leaders and politicians visited Pericles's home all the time, and the young boy would have breathed in the excitement of the discussions about Persia and the new democratic Athens. We have few descriptions of his physical appearance, though the historian Plutarch tells us of Pericles that "physically he was almost perfect, the only exception being his head, which was rather long and out of proportion." An intelligent and serious boy, he

This photo shows the more recent ruins of Athens, Greece. These are landmarks that Pericles is likely to have left behind.

must have picked up information quickly, and he must have been well aware that one day he would be expected, like his father, to play his part in the public life of Athens.

His father, Xanthippus, had been an influential figure in Athens in the 490s and 480s BCE when Athens was facing the threat of a Persian invasion. Indeed, Xanthippus had been in command of the forces that had defeated the Persians at Mycale off the coast of Ionia in 479 BCE, the same day that the Persians had been defeated in Greece itself at the Battle of Plataea. Pericles's mother, Agariste, was around the house almost all the time, and from her, too, he would have picked up many ideas and an awareness of his family's importance. She came from one of the most influential families in Athens, and it was actually her uncle, Cleisthenes, who had introduced democracy to Athens in 507 BCE.

As a little boy, Pericles also saw much of his *paidagogos*, a family slave whose main task was to look after him and see that he came to no harm. In Athens at this time there were more slaves than free Athenians. Certainly the Athenians of the time never thought there was anything wrong in one person owning another person, and valued household slaves had close links to their families. The paidagogos explained to Pericles the importance of good behavior and respect for his elders. But there was time for fun, too. One day they played board games together, the next they were out discovering nature.

Pericles was a spirited boy, and soon more formal teaching was needed for him. By the time he was entering his teens it would have become clear to his parents that this intelligent, inquisitive, strong-willed boy needed rather special teachers.

ATHENIAN EDUCATION

Normally a boy from Pericles's background was educated in three areas. One teacher taught him reading and writing, and he would have learned many passages from the poet Homer, who had written his famous stories of the Trojan Wars. Most Athenians were literate, and Pericles learned to read and to write on wax tablets.

Another teacher introduced the young boy to music, for the Athenians regarded music as an essential part of schooling. They believed that music had a moral effect on pupils. Good music produced upright, loyal citizens. Bad music, on the other hand, had a corrupting influence. Pericles might have learned to play the flute and the lyre, a stringed instrument somewhat like a modern guitar.

A third teacher taught him athletics: running, jumping, throwing the javelin and discus, wrestling, and even boxing. This would take place in the *palaestra*, a square training area with colonnades all round where the boys could rest in the shade. Athletes exercised naked and before starting would coat their bodies with olive oil. After exercise they scraped the oil and grime off and took cold baths.

Athletics were important for two reasons. Many of the state festivals had athletic contests, and a young person from a good family would be expected to compete in them. Furthermore, Athens was a military state, and from an early age Pericles knew the importance of being physically fit and able, if necessary, to fight for his city. Ancient writers do not tell us specifically whether Pericles had this sort of education, but it is very likely that he did. What they do tell us is that his parents, aware that they had a very special son, engaged two very special teachers for him, Damon and Anaxagoras.

PERICLES'S TEACHERS

Damon was Pericles's music teacher, and he had a very strong influence on his pupil. All teachers were expected not just to teach subjects but also to develop qualities of good behavior and character in their pupils. So Damon continued to develop Pericles's knowledge of Homer and also taught him how to sing and play the lyre. He would also want to prepare his young pupil for public life. Damon made Pericles aware of the responsibilities that lay ahead of him as a member of one of the foremost families in Athens. Damon, as well as being a teacher of music, was also interested in philosophy and politics, and he saw his job as preparing Pericles for the contests of political life.

Pericles's other teacher was Anaxagoras, a much more famous Greek than Damon. Anaxagoras came from Clazomenae, one of the Greek towns on the coast of Ionia, in modern Turkey, where men had recently started to ask questions about the great issues of life. Where do we come from? What is the world made of? What is the nature of the stars and the sun and the moon? How ought men to behave toward each other? What can we

This 1875 fresco by the Italian Renaissance artist known as Raphael depicts Athenian students receiving various lessons from their teachers.

learn from mathematics? It was Anaxagoras who encouraged Pericles to ask questions, to search for the natural causes of events, rather than putting everything down to the gods. A story is told how Pericles was once sent a ram's head that had just one central horn, like a unicorn. A soothsayer, who was employed to find religious meanings for strange things like this, said that this meant that Pericles would soon be the one important politician in the city. But Anaxagoras took the ram's head, opened it up, and showed that it was a deformation of the skull that had led to the single horn, nothing to do with the gods but arising from a natural cause. Basically, Anaxagoras taught Pericles not to rely on superstition but to use his common sense.

But Anaxagoras taught Pericles something else that was destined to differentiate him from his contemporaries: how to speak in public. In these days there were few books, as they were very expensive and difficult to keep in the form of clay tablets. So speaking person to person was the normal method of communication. The Athenians loved talking and were famous for it. The spoken word was important in many different areas—in politics, when the people met to make decisions

King Xerxes, Persian rival of Greece, sails to meet the allied forces that resisted him.

on important matters; in the theater, where the audience had to be moved by the playwright's words; in the courts of law; and even at dinner parties, where an Athenian of Pericles's background was expected to talk convincingly about a whole variety of topics. The skills that Pericles showed in his mastery of the art of speaking were greatly admired, and it was Anaxagoras who had shown him the way.

ATHENS IN CONFLICT

Yet perhaps even more important than formal schooling was the atmosphere in Athens during those turbulent days. Only five years old at the time,

THE GRECO-PERSIAN WARS

The Persian Empire had originally set its sights on adding Greece to its territories some time after 499 BCE. At this time, the Persian Empire was under the rule of Darius I, also known as Darius the Great. Greek city-states assisted the Ionians in their rebellion against tyrants appointed by the Persian Empire in those territories, but their rebellion was crushed in 493 BCE.

In the Greco-Persian Wars, rulers of the Persian Empire would attempt to take over all of Greece for the next forty-two years. The first Persian invasion would end at Marathon in a decisive defeat, leaving in its wake a lingering desire to bend Greece to the might of the widest-spread empire to date. Following in the footsteps of Darius I would be his son, Xerxes I, who gathered a massive force of invaders only to be defeated in 479 BCE, eventually resulting in empire forces being chased away from Greece.

Pericles was probably unaware of the great Battle of Marathon, where the Persian expeditionary force was defeated and turned back. But ten years later he would have felt the apprehension in the city as the Persians made preparations in 480 BCE for another mammoth expedition to punish Athens once and for all.

One of Pericles's contemporaries, the historian Herodotus, tells us that the Persian army numbered five million men. Even allowing for gross exaggeration, it must have been a mighty expedition. Gallantly the Greek allies defeated this army and navy in three important battles. At this time, Pericles was about fifteen or sixteen years old. It would have captured his imagination, and it is not hard to imagine him rushing down to greet his father as he sailed back victoriously into the port of Piraeus with his fleet of triremes, or warships. A boy of such spirit must have been itching to fight himself, not least because, with other Athenians, he had suffered the shame of being forced to leave his home in the city and seek refuge on the island of Salamis as the Persian army drew near.

From his teachers Damon and Anaxagoras, and from all the talk at home, Pericles came to realize how these victories had been the result of the bravery and spirit of the ordinary Athenians who fought in the ranks and rowed in the fleet. He would have known that they were fighting not for a

This tombstone depicts Xanthippus, Pericles's highly influential father, who helped the Greeks defeat the invading Persian Empire forces.

king or a tyrant or a few nobles, but for themselves and their own government. Every citizen had a say in all important decisions.

POLITICAL PERICLES

In 477 BCE, Pericles had just come of age. He was eighteen years old and could now engage in Athenian life. For someone of his background, this meant, above all, a political life, but first he would have had a year of military service with the Athenian army. This might have involved guarding one of the forts that protected Athens to the north. Or he may have been involved in one of the campaigns against the Persians in the 470s, when Athens led the other Greek states in a drive to make all the seas around Greece safe from Persian harassment. In later years, Pericles was a renowned general, so it is likely he had plenty of war experience as a young man. He would have gotten to know Cimon, the great commander responsible for laying the foundations of the Athenian Empire. Cimon had served under Pericles's father in the Persian Wars. But campaigning happened only in the summer months, so for much of the year Pericles was home at Athens.

Here for the first time he became actively involved in political life. For some years he was very much an observer, watching, studying how democracy worked, biding his time, learning the skills of a politician, making influential friends.

This colored lithograph by Louis Dupré shows the Temple of Jupiter in the foreground and the Acropolis of Athens in the background.

Once a week or so he walked to the Pnyx, where the Assembly of all adult male Athenians met in the open air. Each time he passed the Acropolis, the striking outcrop of rock that dominates the city, he remembered the temples that used to adorn it and

the new temple to Athena still being built when the Persians attacked. Now, as he made his way up to the Pnyx, all he could see were broken and burnt stones and charred wood, a scene of complete desolation. The Athenians had vowed that until they had eliminated the Persian threat forever, the Acropolis would remain as a bleak memorial of the terrible days when the enemy had entered and sacked their city in 480 BCE. One day, he must have said to himself, I will rebuild those temples!

CHAPTER 2

THE YOUNG POLITICIAN

In democratic Athens, anyone who wanted influence needed the support of the men who were allowed to engage in politics. The changes Pericles would enact would certainly help him to gain popular support, and the environment that Athens faced would also enable the pursuit of his ambitions.

THE COUNCIL

At the Pnyx in the open air, Pericles would have joined several thousand other Athenians to discuss state business and to make decisions. In the streets near the Pnyx were policemen, called Scythian archers, who carried whips dipped in red dye, ready to mark any citizens trying to avoid going to the Assembly. Those marked in this way would be liable for a fine, for it was regarded as a citizen's duty to attend the Assembly. First the members of the Council arrived. There were 500 of them, and their job was to prepare business for the Assembly and to enforce the Assembly's decisions. They were all over thirty years of age and came from all over Ath-

This photo shows the remaining ruins of the Pnyx's speaker's platform, a public outlet for discussing Athenian political life.

ens and Attica. They met each day in the Council House half a mile from the Pnyx. They represented a cross-section of Athenian society, and they were picked by lot in their villages and neighborhoods. The Athenians favored selection by lot. It ensured that a variety of citizens from different classes and backgrounds were in public positions, and it made bribery very difficult.

Perhaps the issue would be the construction of a new road down to the silver mines south of Athens. The Council would have already discussed this and would have produced motions in support of the measure for the ordinary citizens of the Assembly to vote on. Before the Assembly's vote, any Athenian had the right to speak for or against the motion. We know that Pericles tended only to speak on matters that he thought particularly important, so he might not have weighed in on every issue. Also present at the debate were the ten generals, each one of them elected for a year. Their job was to lead the army and the navy, but they were also respected by the people for their opinions on non-military matters. In peacetime, though they had no power to overturn the verdict of the people, they could exert considerable political influence. Pericles would have noticed how even these important Athenians had to persuade the citizens if they wanted anything done. Soon a vote was taken by a show of hands.

This form of direct democracy, where every citizen has his say, is very different from modern democracies, where ordinary citizens are only asked to vote every two or four years, and where laws are approved by elected representatives rather than everyone. Modern states are too big for direct democracy to work, but the Athenian democracy provided the blueprint for all later democracies.

But, even the Athenian democracy had its failings. No women were allowed into the Assembly. They had no political say at all. Slaves were not allowed to take part, and there were more slaves in Athens and Attica than freeborn citizens. Nor

TYPES OF DEMOCRACY

The most basic democracy involves a class of equals called citizens who regularly vote. They may be voting on laws or whether or not to declare war, or they may be voting to choose someone for a job. This is called a direct democracy. A representative democracy, also called a republic, involves voting for someone to represent the people by making and voting on laws, as well as completing the other functions that the voting public chooses for them to do.

A constitutional democracy is a democracy that is guided by rules that remain for each ruling group to follow, whereas a non-constitutional democracy allows for different rules that are based on what those in power decide.

A federal democracy divides power between multiple groups. For example, in the US, a federal government shares power with the states, and the individual people also have a share of power. The power of a unitary democracy, on the other hand, is in the hands of a single group.

Naturally, a democratic government must choose the level of representation, decide whether or not the rulers must observe guidelines and limitations, and determine which groups must share power. Athens, in particular, was a direct federal democracy that didn't have a written constitution, but there was a formal structure of rules that the governing body observed.

Looking at this room full of people, it's clear that the Athenian system of government limited who was allowed to participate.

were foreigners living in Athens allowed to vote, however long they had lived in the city.

The Athenians had another method of checking the ambitions of powerful individuals. They used a system called ostracism. A meeting of the Assembly would decide whether an ostracism should be held, and then all the citizens would write the name of the person that they wanted to leave the city on a small piece of pottery called an ostracon. The pieces of pottery were then counted and the person whose name appeared most often was expelled from the city for ten years. Many of these ostracons have been found in the agora in Athens, including some with the name of Pericles's father and Pericles himself.

It is hard not to admire the Athenian system, especially with hindsight, when we see what the Athenians achieved in the short space of time when they held their empire. Pericles as a young man in his twenties went regularly to the Assembly and saw how important the ordinary Athenian citizen was. Even though he was of noble birth himself, Pericles understood that any future development of Athens must have as its foundation these ordinary Athenians. Above all, these same citizens were the men who manned the Athenian fleet, and the fleet would be at the heart of Athenian success.

CIMON'S TRIUMPH

Throughout the 470s and the 460s BCE, Athens and her allies were still at war against the Persians, both to extract money from them for the cost of the earlier campaigns and to make the Aegean Sea safe for Greek trading. Much of the success of Athens in these campaigns was due to Cimon, an inspired and popular general. Various expeditions that he led had culminated in a mighty victory for the Athenians in 467 BCE at Eurymedon in southern Turkey, where the entire fleet of 200 Persian ships was destroyed. We do not know if Pericles was with the Athenian forces for this battle, but we do know that from this time on the Persians were no longer a serious threat and the Greek cities could start to think in terms of a

This piece by Wilhelm von Kaulbach depicts Greek forces successfully overcoming the Persian Empire's fleet.

peaceful future. Many of the allies who had helped Athens in these campaigns now wanted to disband the army and navy and go home. But Cimon and the other Athenians were unhappy about this, and a number of city-states were now forced by Athens to stay in the alliance. One such state was the island of Thasos, a powerful city in the north Aegean that in 465 BCE revolted against the Athenian alliance. Cimon set about besieging the main town on the island, but he knew that such a siege would keep him away from Athens for years.

ARISTOCRACY OR DEMOCRACY

Pericles was then in his thirties and ready to make his mark on the political scene. He had formed an alliance with an Athenian called Ephialtes, who shared his views about democracy and the importance of including ordinary Athenians in the government of the state. Their natural opponents were Cimon and his supporters, who wanted to keep the more traditional form of government in which an assembly of older and richer Athenians, called the *Areopagus*, made the important decisions. Together Pericles and Ephialtes set about reducing the powers of the Areopagus and transferring them to the Assembly and the Council. There was some opposition to this from members of the upper classes, some of whom had been prosecuted in the courts by Pericles and Ephialtes, and Ephialtes was killed in street fighting. Suddenly, Pericles found himself the man of the hour and, angry at the death of his friend, he led the Assembly to pass the reform measures that would guarantee the power of the ordinary people in Athens. In the excitement of the moment the people forgot about the great successes of Cimon and his development of their empire, and they ostracized him and turned to Pericles as their main leader.

THE MILITARY STATE

From an early age, Pericles knew that he would be expected to fight for his country and that the prospect of death in battle was a very real one. Indeed, throughout his life from 495 BCE to 429 BCE, apart from one notable period from 446 BCE to 431 BCE, Athens was almost continually at war. And yet in Athens the atmosphere was not warlike and there was no feeling of being in a military state.

Athenians went about their daily business, perhaps as craftsmen, shopkeepers, farmers, or traders, and only when a campaign was to be fought did they take up arms, ready to march or sail to wherever they were commanded. They knew that the price of keeping an empire was to be ready to defend it. And normally a campaign would last for only a few months in the summer.

The Athenian army was made up almost entirely of its better-off citizens. As a hoplite, or infantryman, you had to be rich enough to afford body armor: a bronze helmet, breastplate, and leg armor. There was no central government supply of these necessary items. Much of the training for fighting was done during the year of military service that a citizen had to undergo when he was eighteen, and there is little evidence of regular military combat training beyond this. Indeed, Pericles himself said when addressing the Athenian people:

> We do not have to spend our time practicing to meet sufferings that are still in the future. We meet danger voluntarily with an easy mind, instead of with laborious training.

This attitude produced a real sense of pride in the Athenian hoplite. He fought in line, and with his shield he protected both himself and the person next to him. So all those fighting in the line were dependent on each other, and this led to a readiness to risk one's life for the man next to you. Even without regular training, the Athenian hoplites were a force to be reckoned with and won many battles in Pericles's time.

MEASURING ATHENIAN MIGHT

The city-state that opposed Athens for much of this period was Sparta. Sparta was a military state in the mountains of the Peloponnese 140 miles (225 kilometers) south of Athens. Here, Spartan boys were brought up from their earliest youth to regard war and fighting as the only things that really mattered, and all their education was geared toward military training. Their way of life was simple. All the citizens, a group consisting solely of men, were permanently in the army. While much of their time was spent in keeping the city-states around them under their control, they would also venture out of their home area from time to time to engage in expeditions abroad. They had helped Athens to defeat the Persians in 480 BCE. The Athenians might be spirited fighters, but everyone in Greece knew that the Spartan hoplite was supreme. Above all, everyone remembered the famous 300 Spartans who under their king Leonidas had fought to the death at the Pass of Thermopylae, holding off the huge army of Xerxes, king of Persia.

But there was one area where Athens had no equal, and that was its navy. In 483 BCE, a farsighted leader named Themistocles had persuaded the Athenians to use a rich vein of silver that they had found in the mines south of Athens to build a fleet of

200 ships, and this provided the basis for Athenian power. No one was more aware of the importance of this fleet than Pericles himself. Many times he

This oil painting from circa 1860 depicts youths participating in the *agoge* system of education. It took young, underage Spartans to adulthood and prepared them for war.

must have mounted his horse in the center of Athens and ridden down to Piraeus, the great port of Athens some five miles (eight kilometers) away. He would have galloped out of the Dipylon, or Double Gate, down a long straight road with defensive walls on either side. This road linked Athens to its naval base. At Piraeus, there were three naval harbors and a thriving commercial port. Two of the naval harbors were shaped like horseshoes and surrounded by sheds where the Athenian warships were docked. Each ship had its individual shed and the foundations of some of these can still be seen today. All around were warehouses storing equipment for the ships—masts, sails, oars, and ropes.

NAVAL OPERATIONS

The Athenian warship was called a trireme. It had three banks of oars manned by 170 oarsmen. Above the rowing levels, there was a flat deck where up to twenty marines stood ready to board enemy ships if necessary, or to repel boarders. About 100 feet (30 meters) long and only 9 feet (3 meters) wide, the trireme was basically a floating guided missile. At the bow was a bronze ram head, and the aim in fighting was to drive this into the side of an enemy ship and sink it. Recently, a reconstruction of a trireme was built in Athens, and sea trials have proved what a lethal weapon it was.

It is often mistakenly thought that these ships were rowed by slaves, as was the case with oared galleys from Roman times onward. This was not so. The Athenian triremes were rowed by free men, either Athenian citizens or their allies. The citizens were those same people who supported Pericles in the Assembly and who Pericles knew were essential to Athens's success. In cramped conditions and with great discomfort, unable to see anything but the back of the rower in front of him, the Athenian oarsman knew two things—he was the best oarsman in the world and he was his own master.

It must have been an amazing sight when those 200 ships, manned by 34,000 oarsmen, were at sea each with their 170 oars all moving in perfect rhythm. Foreign visitors to the city would have been in no doubt about the nature of Athens's power and supremacy. The historian Thucydides described a huge expedition—at least 100 warships with many transport ships, too—that sailed for Sicily some time after Pericles's death:

When the ships were manned and everything had been taken aboard, silence was commanded by the sound of a trumpet, and the custom-

ary prayers made before putting to sea were offered up, not by each ship separately but by them all together following the words of a herald. The

These Greek triremes are fighting to destroy each other's boats. Once a boat is destroyed, the fighters are stranded in the water, making them easy prey.

> crowds on the shore also, the citizens and others who wished well to the expedition, joined together in the prayers. Then when the hymn had been sung, they put out to sea, first sailing out in column, and then racing each other as far as the island of Aegina.

These then were the forces that were available to Athens in the middle of the fifth century BCE, but it was the political scene in Athens that would set them to war.

CHAPTER 3

WAR

It seemed that for Pericles, the two main functions of a state were to wage war with enemies and to beautify the country. Considering the great amount of destruction that war often brought, it's not surprising that he would see fit to add as many structures as he was able to gain support for. What some non-Athenians may have found surprising, however, was how he attempted to gain that support.

POLITICS IN ATHENS

It must have been with some surprise that Pericles found himself the main political leader in Athens in 461 BCE. He might have expected to have Ephialtes sharing the responsibility with him, but Ephialtes had been assassinated and there was unlikely to be any strong opposition to his leadership, as Cimon

This 1878 illustration depicts the return of Cimon after his ten years of ostracization.

had just been ostracized for ten years. Pericles was relatively free to pursue the policies he wanted. He not only wanted to increase the size of Athens's empire abroad, he also wanted to extend Athens's power nearer to the city.

A number of military actions over the next ten years make it clear that he hoped to develop a land empire that would include Megara, a town some thirty miles (forty-eight kilometers) from Athens on the Isthmus of Corinth, and also the state of Boeotia to the north of Athens. But he never lost sight of the importance of Athens's naval power. At the heart of his policy was the idea that Athens and her port should be as formidable and closely linked as possible. With this in mind, he set about building a third long wall to connect Athens with Piraeus even more securely.

ATHENS AND ENEMIES

In 460 BCE, Pericles sent off a large expedition of 200 ships to Cyprus and Egypt. Egypt had been part of the Persian Empire for a long time. At first the expedition was successful, but soon it was unable to make any further progress up the Nile River. At home, Athens came into conflict with a number of her neighbors when she decided to form an alliance with Megara. The two states most upset by this were Corinth, also situated on the isthmus, thirty miles (forty-eight kilometers) from Megara, and Sparta. Over the next fifteen years, there were a number of clashes between Athens and these two states. Pericles was never slow to send forces out to look after Athenian interests.

Pericles also decided to permanently subdue the island of Aegina, which was an old enemy, visible from the coast of Athens. Indeed, Pericles had referred to it sometime earlier as "the eye-sore of Piraeus." Even the disastrous end to the Egyptian expedition in 454 BCE, with virtually no survivors returning to Athens, did not deter the Athenians. They continued to fight with their neighbors to the north in Boeotia and to the south in the Peloponnese. At sea, the Athenians were almost always victorious. When they fought on land, they often came off worse.

At times the Athenian forces were massively overstretched, so much so that on one occasion they had to dispatch a force composed entirely of old men and boys under the age of eighteen to fight and win against the Corinthians in 459 BCE. This engagement was destined to have important consequences, for it ended with the Athenians penning up the Corinthian forces in a small enclosure and pelting them all to death. The Corinthians would never forget the shame and the brutality of this action. Finally in 446 BCE, Athens's most important ally, the island of Euboea, some fifty miles (eighty kilometers) north of Athens, revolted from the alliance and declared its independence. Pericles himself went out with a force of hoplites, suppressed the revolt, and forced the people of Euboea to stay in the empire.

The years 461 BCE to 446 BCE were difficult for Athens, and it is not always easy to see why Pericles was prepared to take so many risks and fight on so many different fronts. There were moments when the Spartans and their allies could have broken Athens's power if they had been prepared to take the initiative. It was a close-run thing, and from this point on, while ensuring that the empire held together, Pericles developed a more cautious policy toward Corinth and Sparta and their allies. Peace was made with Corinth and Sparta in 446 BCE, and this complemented a peace that had been made three years earlier with the Persians. Suddenly, after years of fighting, both against Persia and her Greek neighbors, Athens was finally no longer at war. Pericles was coming up on his fiftieth birthday, and he had an important job to do.

PERICLES REACHES OUT

Pericles had achieved much in the years up to 446 BCE, but he now embarked on the program that was to ensure that his name and the name of Athens would never be forgotten. Now was the time to ensure that in peace Athens would achieve even more than in war.

Athens in 446 BCE was a city unlike any other. Crowds from all over the known world mingled in the streets of the city and its port, Piraeus. The Athenian people themselves felt a new confidence after their wars with the Persians and the other Greek city-states, but they were not overconfident. There had been losses in battle, and many families had lost sons in the fighting. With peace gained, the multitude of oarsmen who manned the fleet were no longer required to serve the warships full-time, and they were looking for other work. New buildings had sprung up in the narrow confines of the city walls—public buildings, shops, and shrines to the gods. In Piraeus a corn exchange and a market had been constructed, and the town around the port itself had been built up with planned streets running at right angles, wide and easy for transport. But one place still stood desolate and in ruins nearly fifty years after it had been burned by the Persians—the Acropolis.

Now was the time to rebuild these temples and to make the Acropolis a marvel for all time. Pericles had been thinking about this all his adult life. Almost every day since he had become a leader, Pericles must have been waiting for the right moment. He would need a good architect, the best in the world, and he would need many skilled craftsmen from all over the Greek world, and even more laborers. He would need money and he would need peace to enable the work to go ahead without interruption. At hand he had the services of those citizens who had been under his command in the fleet and were now looking for new employment.

In an attempt to bring the Greek city-states together, Pericles had proposed a motion in the

This illustration depicts a view of the Acropolis circa 420 BCE in all its glory, restored by Pericles after Persian Empire forces burned it down.

Assembly two years earlier in 448 BCE, a year after peace was made with Persia. This motion invited all the Greek cities to send delegates to a grand meeting at Athens. The matters to be discussed were the Greek temples that had been burned down, not just in Athens but all over the Greek world, as well as the whole question of the security of the seas. However, even though invitations were sent out, the Spartans were already beginning to fear the growth of Athenian power, and under their influence all the other states refused the invitation. Perhaps they all knew that what was really at stake was not just new buildings for Athens, but also a tacit acknowl-

edgement of Athens's leading status. So Athens would have to go it alone.

HONORING THE PATRON GODDESS

The first task was to build a new temple to Athena, the patron goddess of the city. For forty-five years she had been without a proper home, and this temple had to outshine all other temples in Greece. To ensure that all went smoothly, a director of buildings was appointed who was a friend of Pericles's, the sculptor Pheidias. The architects for the great new temple were to be Callicrates and Ictinus. Individual architects were appointed for other buildings. There must have been many discussions before the first stone was laid. But the deciding factor in any argument was always that it must be the very best possible.

BUILDING MATERIALS

The main building materials of Athens were clay, stone, and wood. Red clay was used to make bricks and pottery.

There were widespread deposits of clay throughout Greece, but the clay of Athens may have been from the outskirts of Athens.

Stone, specifically marble, was available in abundance. It came from marble quarries called Pentelikon and Hymettos, and these were close enough to Athens that marble was highly accessible.

Wood wasn't abundant, so it was imported from Macedonia or Thrace when Athenians needed it for heavy construction, or it came from Mt. Parnes.

Typical construction projects included building houses, municipal buildings, and temples. Houses were simple buildings of a structure that municipal buildings would initially follow. The base of a house consisted of rubble stones. Its floor consisted of clay, and the roof was built of terracotta tile. Within the house, wood was used for joists and rafters. Wooden doors for houses were crafted from imported wood.

Starting in the fifth century BCE, the structures of municipal buildings became more substantial, and their walls began to be constructed of sun-dried brick. Occasionally, walls of stone supplied an extravagant touch to a building.

Temples were made mostly of stone, a sign that they were of high importance. This may have been a sign of reverence to the gods or a means of protecting the treasury that was often stored in temples.

And so the Parthenon of Athena began to rise from the volcanic rock of the Acropolis. People were amazed to see the shining white marble blocks of stone as they were pulled along specially made roads from Mount Pentelicon by teams of oxen. Temples in those days were normally built of limestone or sandstone. Marble was far more difficult to work with and cost almost ten times more than ordinary stone.

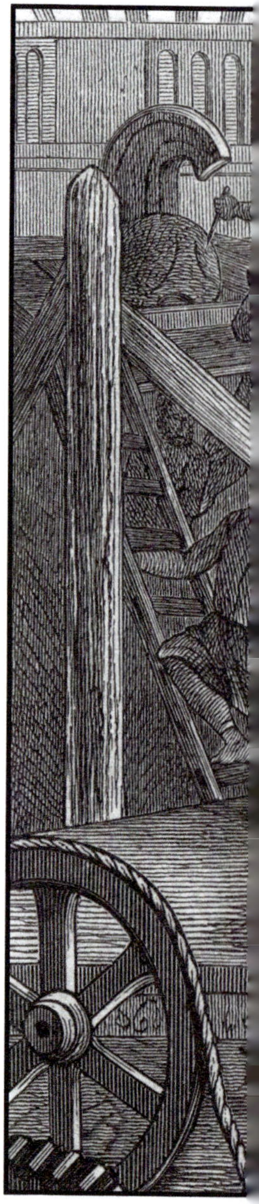

Slowly the partly carved blocks were hauled up onto the Acropolis, where skilled craftsmen and sculptors waited to work on them. Accounts of wages paid to workmen showed how free citizens, foreign workers, and slaves worked side by side. Many of those workers would be the oarsmen, who with peace were no longer required to row all the time. They had fought to build the Athenian Empire. Now they were competing to make what they thought of as the most beautiful temple in the world.

The task facing Callicrates and Ictinus, the Parthenon's designers, was not an easy one. In line with tradition, the temple was rectangular with a row of circular columns on all four sides supporting the roof. There also had to be

This illustration depicts the Parthenon being constructed by paid workers and slaves circa 440 BCE.

a large interior room that would house a huge statue of Athena, and another room to hold the treasures of the goddess. There had to be sculptures on the temple to illustrate Athena's life and her relationship with the Athenian people. The temple had to be large enough to be truly impressive in its own right. It had to have the most secure of foundations and be visible from miles away.

But all these problems were overcome, and within five years the Parthenon stood on the Acropolis, marking the power of the city and the devotion of the Athenians to their goddess.

ATHENA'S PARTHENON

The Parthenon was 210 feet (70 meters) long by 100 feet (30 meters) wide, and the entrance faced east. From the outside the marble would have shined brilliantly in the sun, but if you looked up you would have seen painted carvings decorating the temple. Most impressive would have been those in the pediments or triangular areas at the top of the columns at each end. One showed the birth of Athena. In Athenian myth, she was supposed to have sprung fully armed from the head of Zeus, her father. At the other end in the pediment was a depiction of the contest between Athena and the sea god, Poseidon, to decide who should control Athens and Attica. The story goes that Athena offered the people the olive tree and so won their loyalty.

Two other features have caught the imagination of visitors ever since. As visitors go up the steps into the temple, above their heads inside the columns was a continuous carving 600 feet (200 meters) long that showed a stately procession to Athena, honoring the day each year when a new robe was offered by the people to their goddess. This frieze still exists and is in the British Museum in London. Copies of it exist all round the world, and it is famous for the nobility and realism of its carvings. But even more impressive than this was the huge statue of Athena, thirty feet high, seated on her throne inside the dimly lit temple and shining with gold and ivory. Pheidias, the sculptor of Zeus at Olympia, made this statue and constructed it with plates of gold. The statue was pillaged many centuries ago and now we only have small copies of it that date from Roman times.

There is no doubt that Pericles saw the worship of Athena as central to the future of Athens. Each

This clay carving depicts Athena (*left*) offering the people of Athens (*right*) an olive tree.

year she had her own festival that started with a procession from the Kerameikos, or funeral area of Athens at the Dipylon Gate. The procession moved through the agora past all the most important official buildings in Athens, and then wound its way up to the Acropolis. It is no surprise that Pheidias chose to portray this procession so wonderfully in the Parthenon frieze. It contained horsemen, hoplites, officials, and flute players, and animals being led to sacrifice. The festival itself included an exciting night race with runners carrying torches, followed the next day by competitions and contests and more sacrifices. Over a hundred animals were sacrificed, and every four years when the great festival to Athena was celebrated the contests and sacrifices were even more elaborate.

BUILDING UP ATHENS

The Parthenon was just part of a much bigger building program. This included a grand ceremonial entrance to the Acropolis called the Propylaea, which would also act as a picture gallery for the best of Athenian paintings. It was built after the Parthenon was completed.

This photo of the ruins of the Propylaea overlooks modern-day Athens and the mountains at the opposite side of the city.

An incident, which Plutarch relates, tells of the close interest that Pericles took in the actual building. A craftsman working at a great height slipped and fell to the ground. He lay there severely injured and the doctors told Pericles that the man was unlikely to recover. But the goddess Athena appeared to Pericles in a dream and suggested a course of treatment. He saw that the course of treatment was given to the man, who quickly recovered. In due course Pericles had a statue of Athena the Healer set up on the Acropolis to commemorate the event.

All over Attica splendid temples and public buildings were rising. Pericles wanted everyone in Attica to feel part of this Athenian renaissance. Some of these buildings were in small villages, some on the borders with Boeotia, some by the sea. The most famous is the Temple of Poseidon at Sunium on the southernmost tip of Attica. Poseidon was the god of the sea and second in importance only to Athena for the Athenians. The remains of his gleaming white marble temple stand high above the sea and can still be seen by sailors as a notable landmark from miles away. Below the temple, hewn out of the rock of the cliff face, was a boatshed for two fast rowing boats that could be launched at a moment's notice to bring news of any dangers to the city. Pericles was always aware that Athens must protect her territories and protect these beautiful, new buildings.

Not surprisingly, some people were envious of Pericles's achievements, and up until 443 BCE he was attacked in the Assembly because of the apparent extravagance of the building program. After 443 BCE, there was little criticism of Pericles himself, but his opponents had no hesitation about attacking his friends. Rumors flew around about Pheidias. People claimed that he had cheated the state when making the gold and ivory statue of Athena for the Parthenon. Plutarch tells us that he died in prison either of sickness or after being poisoned. However, as long as the buildings still stood, Pheidias's reputation would be secure.

CHAPTER 4

THE GOLDEN YEARS

Athenian culture was a multifaceted experience, consisting of entertainment, politics, and clear-cut class- and gender-based societal roles. Pericles had a particularly influential hand in influencing the first of those two things, entertainment and politics. Gender roles would be too static of an expectation for him to affect, although in his own personal life, he did what he could.

ATHENIAN DRAMA

It is no coincidence that Athens's greatest playwrights all flourished at the time when Pericles was leading Athens. The greatest of all, Sophocles, was a personal friend of Pericles's throughout their lives. Just as the great buildings are still admired in Athens and Attica, the plays of Sophocles are still produced all over the world, sometimes in the original Greek, but more often in translation. Their plots are based on myths or ancient stories handed down from generation to generation. The most famous of these concerns Oedipus, the king of the

This image shows the chorus performing in one of the final scenes of *Oedipus Rex*.

city of Thebes. These plays are known as tragedies, and they usually tell the story of how men or women as a result of some flaw in their characters or some stroke of bad luck undergo terrible sufferings handed out by the gods or fate. It has even been suggested that Sophocles had Pericles in mind when he wrote the story of Oedipus.

Certainly in another of his great tragedies, *Antigone*, Sophocles discusses the conflict between the interests of the state and the individual. Antigone's brother has been fighting for the enemy against her own country. He dies and Antigone sees it as her duty to give him a proper burial. But the king of her state, Creon, has ordered that none of the enemy are to be buried. They must be left to rot on the battlefield, and anyone who defies this order will be executed. The strength of Pericles's influence must have been clear to everyone in Athens, and to many, Sophocles's treatment of the story of Antigone would have seemed very relevant.

FOOD

The staples of the Athenian diet were barley bread and wheat. The land wasn't plentiful and fertile enough to grow enough wheat to feed everyone, so food was also imported. Supplementary to Greek diets was olive oil, olives, grapes, wine, figs, milk, cheese, grain, fruits, vegetables, and cakes.

This illustration portrays a banquet, an event that featured food and entertainment. However, meals in ancient Athens were usually a private, domestic affair.

While meat was also a part of the Greek diet, it wasn't a meal unto itself. Greeks were against killing animals just for food, but if they killed an animal for a sacrifice, they then felt it was justified to eat some of the animal. Myth has it that ancient Greeks may have sacrificed humans and cannabalized them as well.

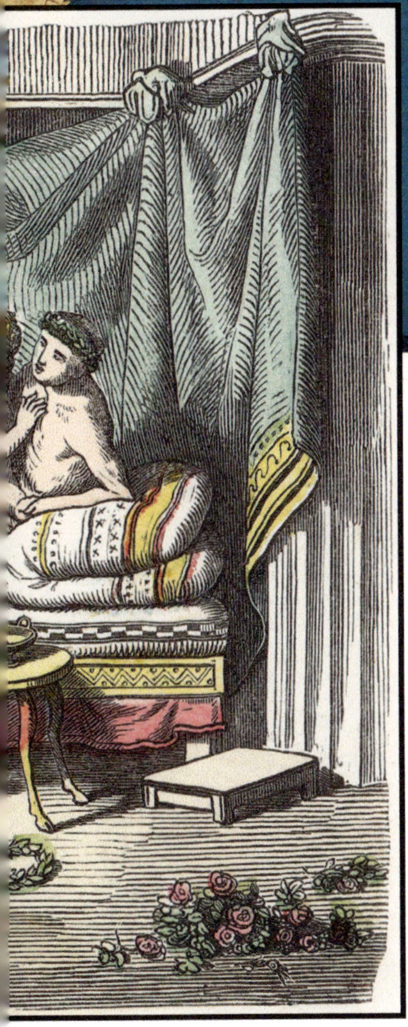

Apart from the tragedies, comedies were also performed, with fantastic plots, slapstick humor, and comments on topical events in Athens. Aristophanes was the most famous of the comic poets, and he was quite likely to attack leading figures at Athens in his plays. Anything was acceptable in these comedies and there is no doubt that they were very popular with the ordinary people. But they had an underlying seriousness and often dealt with themes like the ordinary person's dislike of war. In one well-known passage, Aristophanes attacks Pericles after his death for being too keen to fight with the Spartans. By the late 430s BCE, the storm clouds of war were hovering over the city again.

THEATER

Certainly drama was immensely important for the Athenians. Plays were produced only as part of a festival. The Athenians did not have weekends, and instead their year was broken up by a series of major festival days, up to sixty or seventy in number. Pericles realized the importance of relaxation for the Athenians, and in his famous funeral speech, delivered in 430 BCE, he said:

> When our work is over we are in a position to enjoy all kinds of recreation for our spirits. There are various kinds of contests and sacrifices regularly throughout the year. In our own homes we find a beauty and

good taste that delight us every day and drives away our cares.

Originally most of the festivals were connected to the growing of crops and the harvest, but by the fifth century BCE, they were more important as times of relaxation for the people. Plays were put on at two great festivals, the *Dionysia* in March, and the *Lenaea* in December.

This nineteenth-century chromolithograph depicts people celebrating Anthesteria, a festival in honor of Dionysus.

Theater buildings had no roofs. In fact, in the earliest times the audience would just sit on a hillside and look down on the performers below. At Athens the theater was set into the south side of the Acropolis and could hold 17,000 people. Plays would begin soon after dawn and go on for seven hours. At first the seats were wooden benches and this would have been so in the time of Pericles. Later, stone was used as the theaters became more permanent. The horseshoe shape of the Greek theater is famous. Many of them were taken over by

This wide shot of Odeion of Herodes Atticus shows ample seating room for the events held here.

the Romans and can still be visited today. Right next door to the theater in Athens was the concert hall, or Odeion, that was built by Pericles. It was a covered building with a high roof that was said by comedians to reflect the shape of Pericles's own head. Inside the Odeion singing and musical contests were held.

There was considerable excitement on the days of the dramatic festivals. These festivals took the form of competitions between three playwrights with a group of ten ordinary people chosen to act as judges. Just as the Athenian people were very good at listening to arguments in the Assembly, they were skilled at understanding complicated themes and ideas in the plays. Actors wore masks so there were no facial expressions visible, and the words and their delivery were all-important.

Women did not act. All the female roles were played by men.

LIFE FOR WOMEN

What was domestic life like for Pericles? What was his wife like? For anyone writing today these would be important issues when dealing with an eminent statesman. But ancient writers were not really concerned with these matters. We do not even know the name of Pericles's wife. We know that she had been married before, and that she had been the mother of an influential friend of Pericles's, Callias. She gave birth to two sons, Xanthippus, named after Pericles's father, and Paralus, but then they separated and she lived with another man. It seems as though the separation was agreed to by both of them, and there is no word of a divorce.

There was one woman who was very important in Pericles's life apart from his wife. This was Aspasia, who had been born in Miletus in Ionia and who became a close friend and lover of Pericles. It is likely that she was a highly intelligent person, and Plutarch talks about her "rare political wisdom" and goes on to say how Pericles lived with

Aspasia "and loved her dearly." Again, personal enemies of Pericles tried to get at him by attacking Aspasia. On one occasion when she was prosecuted in the courts for a religious offense, Pericles is said to have burst into tears in the court and begged the jurors to let Aspasia off.

More generally speaking, an Athenian mother or wife seems to have had a very restricted life, with virtually no education and no real say in how the city was run. This may seem strange to us when we consider that the patron goddess of the city, Athena, was female, and that the plays of the time were full of strong female characters. It is likely that although women were not allowed to play a formal part in the public life of Athens, they nonetheless had a lot of influence over their husbands and children. Had they always been completely in the background, as some writers have suggested, it seems unlikely that the Athenians could have achieved so much in as many areas.

While women had very little to do with the political and commercial life of Athens, at home they had considerable importance in managing the household. This would include the making of clothes, the provision of food, the cooking, the

This illustration depicts an ancient Greek family in a place of worship.

management of slaves within the household, and the upbringing of the children in the early years. It is clear from Greek literature and from tender scenes on gravestones that relations between husband and wife were often close and affectionate. But the fact remains that for women it was a very different life from what we consider acceptable. For example, when there were dinner parties at the better-off homes, wives were not present. The men would have dinner and then discuss politics or philosophy or lighter topics, and they might be entertained by other women, but the wives would remain behind the scenes. In a wealthier home, part of the house was reserved for women and they were expected to keep to this area. There was no formal education for girls and they would have learned from their mothers only what they needed to know to run a household. Women did have their own special religious festivals where men were not present, but it is unlikely that in Pericles's time they went to the theater, and they certainly did not go to the Assembly.

And yet we know from writers and from scenes on pottery that home life went on, families were brought up, and the family was thought of by most Athenians as being very important. It is still surprising, though, that when Pericles described the glories of Athens at the end of the first year of war with Sparta, his only words were: "Your greatest glory is not to be inferior to what God has made you, and the greatest glory of a woman is to be least talked about by men, whether they are praising you or criticizing you."

CHAPTER 5

GATHERING CLOUDS

War and disease: this was the world Pericles was immersed in at the time of his death. He had clear strategies for how to overcome the enemies that he led Athens into taking on, but he would not be there to see them through. While his military vision couldn't continue beyond his death, the creative works he had commissioned throughout his life would live on.

QUIET GROWS INTO CONFLICT

The years from 446 BCE to 431 BCE had been great ones for Athens. During that period Pericles had been elected as a *strategos*, or general, every year, and his influence with the Athenian people was at its peak. Athens's powers had hardly been challenged, and there had been only one serious

This 1837 David d'Angers statue depicts Philopoemen, a skilled Greek general who served as strategos for eight years.

revolt among its allies when the island of Samos, off the south coast of Turkey, took up arms in 440 BCE. Pericles himself led the Athenian forces as commander, and after a bitter campaign laid siege to the main city on the island. Nine months later, Samos surrendered. Much more typical of this period was the expedition that Pericles made to the Black Sea to show off Athenian power and to establish Athenian influence with the local princes there. The Black Sea area was important for the Athenians as much of their corn and their wood for building ships came from there.

However, after 431 BCE, the Spartans were becoming increasingly worried about the power and ambitions of the Athenians. During the years of peace, the Spartans had watched with growing resentment as the Athenians secured their hold on the Aegean Sea and its rich commerce while continuing to receive tribute or taxes from all the coastal cities. The city of Corinth, too, had become envious of Athens's success, and her citizens also still wanted to get revenge for the brutal slaughter of her soldiers in 459 BCE. Even in Athens itself there was a certain degree of restlessness. For some ten years now the navy had seen no important action, and it was unlike the Athenian oarsmen to be happy with that. Pericles himself saw war coming. Aristophanes, the comedy writer, suggested that Pericles was responsible for the outbreak of war. In fact, there were a number of causes. There was a general feeling from 435 BCE that war was not far away.

INCREASING PRESSURE

The historian Thucydides provides a brief sum-

AGGRESSIONS AND ALLIANCES

Similar to more recent global conflicts, the Peloponnesian War started a long way from the main players Athens and Sparta. Corcyra (modern Corfu), a state on the northwest coast of Greece that had been founded 200 years previously by Corinth, came into conflict with her mother city. Fearing that they would be defeated by the stronger forces of Corinth, the people of Corcyra asked Athens for help. Athens might well have refused, but the Athenians did not like the idea of Corinth taking over the navy of Corcyra. It was the strongest in the area after the Athenian and Corinthian navies at this time. The Athenians chose to form a defensive

This 1887 Victor Duruy illustration depicts the valley of Sparta, land of the long-time rivals of the Athenians.

alliance with Corcyra and sent out a small detachment of ships to help.

The Corinthians were not amused. They put pressure on Sparta to help and to declare war. At first the Spartans hesitated. One of the kings of Sparta at the time was actually a personal friend of Pericles's and was not keen to get embroiled in a long and costly war. The Spartans stalled for a couple of years. But when Athens treated her neighboring city, Megara, with considerable arrogance, refusing to allow the Megarians any access to Athenian markets, Sparta became more willing to consider war. By this time Athens was also becoming embroiled in a conflict with one of her allies in northwest Greece, Potidaea, and now the idea of war became a real possibility for Sparta and her Peloponnesian allies.

mary of the fifty years between the Persian wars and the Peloponnesian War and then goes into the causes of the Peloponnesian War in considerable detail. His account includes the debate at Sparta when Corinth and other allies tried to persuade Sparta to declare war. An Athenian was present and spoke arrogantly about Athens's power. The pressure from her allies on Sparta was intense, so Sparta finally declared war on Athens.

Did Pericles and the Athenians want a war at this time? Certainly it is hard not to see some of Athens's actions as being provocative and calculated to upset the states in the Peloponnese. Furthermore, Pericles was very clear about how the war should be fought, and Thucydides recounts one of his speeches where he tells the Athenians what they must do, both in preparation for the war and in their conduct of it. While Thucydides does not claim to be repeating the exact words of Pericles in speeches like these, there is no doubt that the style, tone, and content ring true:

> Sea power is of enormous importance. Look at it this way. Suppose we were an island, would we not be absolutely secure from attack? As it is we must try to think of ourselves as islanders; we must abandon our land and our houses, and safeguard the sea and the city. We must not join battle on land with the greatly superior forces of the Peloponnesians . . . I could give you many other reasons why you should feel confident in ultimate victory, if only you will make up your minds not

> to add to the empire while the war is still in progress, and not to go out of your way to involve yourselves in new perils . . . We must realize that the war is being forced upon us, and the more readily we accept the challenge the less eager to attack us will our opponents be. We must realize, too, that, both for cities and for individuals, it is from the greatest dangers that the greatest glory is to be won. When our fathers stood against the Persians they had no such resources as we have now. Indeed, they abandoned even what they had, and then it was by wisdom rather than good fortune, by daring rather than by material power, that they drove back the foreign invasion and made our city what it is today. We must live up to the standard they set. We must resist our enemies in any and every way, and try to leave to those who come after us an Athens that is as great as ever.

This passage gives us some idea of Pericles's

range as a speaker, appealing to both the minds and the emotions of his listeners.

THE WAR AND THE PLAGUE

In the first year of the war, 431 BCE, there was little activity. The Spartans moved into Attica in early summer and burned the Athenian crops and olive trees. The Athenians responded by boarding their triremes and making attacks on various points of the Peloponnesian coast. Finally, toward autumn, the Athenians, once they knew that the Spartans had gone home for the winter, moved into the Isthmus of Megara and destroyed the land around the city. There were casualties, but not very many, and at the end of the year Pericles followed the custom of walking down to the Kerameikos, the funeral area, and making a speech praising those who had died in the first year of the war. This speech has come to be seen as an idealized picture of Periclean Athens and a few quotations will give the flavor of it:

> Let me say that our system of government does not copy the institutions of our neighbors. It is more a case of our being a model to others,

This illustration shows Pericles delivering his funeral oration after the first year of the Peloponnesian War.

than of our imitating anyone else. Our constitution is called a democracy because power is in the hands not of a minority but of the whole people . . . We are free and tolerant in our private lives; but in public affairs we keep to the law. This is because it commands our deep respect . . . Our city is open to the world . . . Our love of what is beautiful does not lead to extravagance; our love of the things of the mind does not make us soft. We regard wealth as something to be properly used, rather than as something to boast about. As for poverty, no one need be ashamed to admit it: The real shame is not taking practical measures to escape from it. Here each individual is interested not only in his own affairs but in the affairs of the state as well. Even those who are mostly occupied with their own business are extremely well-informed on general politics. This is

> a peculiarity of ours: We do not say that a man who takes no interest in politics is a man who minds his own business; we say that he has no business here at all . . . Taking everything together then I declare that our city is an education to Greece.

Pericles had considered every possibility in his preparations for the conflict with the Peloponnesians, but what happened next could have come straight out of a Greek tragedy. An outbreak of plague hit Athens. Thucydides describes it in detail and it is clear that the disease, which supposedly originated in Egypt, was particularly virulent:

> People in perfect health suddenly began to have burning feelings in the head; their eyes became inflamed and red; inside their mouths there was bleeding from the throat and tongue . . . inside the body there was a feeling of burning, so that people could not bear the touch of even the lightest linen clothing but wanted to be completely naked. And indeed

most of all would have liked to
plunge into cold water.

Thucydides goes on to describe the despair

This nineteenth-century engraving depicts the suffering of the afflicted during the Plague of Athens.

that affected anyone who caught the disease and the way that the crowded conditions in the city contributed to the speed of its advance. Even worse was the ensuing lawlessness and disregard for normal ways of behaving. It was every man for himself, and it is clear that the whole way of life in Athens came close to breaking down. Such was the fear of the disease that the Spartans abandoned their invasion of Attica early in the summer of 430 BCE and returned home, terrified of contracting it. One further result was that for the first time in his life the people of Athens blamed Pericles for their terrible situation. It was he who had persuaded them to retire behind their walls and not take on the Spartans in open battle. Crowded inside the city in cramped conditions, they were a natural prey to the disease.

Nonetheless, Pericles saw

that the war must go on. Indeed, he may have felt that people would have a better chance of survival away from Athens. He led a naval force to attack various towns on the Peloponnese and returned home in late summer 430 BCE. There he found that as a result of the Spartan attacks on Attica and the depression caused by the plague, the Athenians had turned against him. He was deposed as strategos and forced to pay a fine. Even so they still elected him strategos for the year 429 BCE.

THE DEATH OF PERICLES

Early in 429 BCE Pericles came down with a serious illness, though it was not the plague that had hit the city the year before. Plutarch describes it as "a kind of dull, lingering fever, which persisted through a number of different symptoms and gradually wasted his bodily strength and undermined his noble spirit." As he lay dying, friends and notable Athenians came to visit him. The visitors gathered around his deathbed and, imagining him to be unconscious, talked about his great achievements: his nine victories as an Athenian commander, his virtue, the extent of his power, and his famous exploits. Pericles had actually been following what they were saying and suddenly spoke. He was astonished, he said, that they should praise him for his exploits, which owed at least as much to good fortune as to his own efforts, and anyway other generals had done equally well. Yet they said nothing of his greatest and most glorious claim to fame. "I mean by this" he went on, "that no Athenian ever put on mourning because of me."

These last years had not been easy ones for Pericles. His friends had come under attack, his two sons had died of the plague, and he himself had for a time lost the confidence of the Athenian people. One of the last things he did before succumbing to his illness was to ask the Athenian people to pass a bill that would legitimize his son by his lover Aspasia. The people agreed to this, and the boy was formally registered as an Athenian citizen and later even became an Athenian general.

WHAT HE LEFT BEHIND

The death of Pericles marked the end of an era, and even though his policies were continued in Athens's

This portrait offers a visualization of what Pericles's lover Aspasia may have looked like.

fight against Sparta over the next ten years, his personality and leadership were enormously missed. He had dominated politics in Athens like no other person from 460 BCE to 430 BCE, and he had masterminded both the consolidation of the Athenian Empire and the final development of democracy in the city. But he had done something more than this. He had created a climate in Athens that encouraged writers, artists, and craftsmen to flourish as in no other ancient Greek city. For this judgement we do not have to rely on a biographer like Plutarch or a historian like Thucydides. We have the original texts of the plays, the original sculptures, and the ruins of the temples to make our own assessment.

Even so, Thucydides should have the last word. For he had known Pericles and was aware of his greatness. After acknowledging the quality of Pericles's leadership and the greatness of Athens at the time, he continues:

> Pericles, because of his position, his intelligence, and his known integrity, could respect the liberty of the people and at the same time hold it in check. It was he who led them, rather than they who led him, and

> since he never sought power from any wrong motive, he was under no necessity of flattering them. In fact he was so highly respected that he was able to speak angrily to them and to contradict them. Certainly when he saw that they were going too far in a mood of overconfidence, he would bring back to them a sense of their dangers; and when they were discouraged for no good reason he would restore their confidence. So, in what was nominally a democracy, power was really in the hands of the first citizen.

It is a powerful tribute and a true one.

Acropolis A rocky hill in the center of Athens on which the Parthenon is situated.

Aegean Sea Part of the Mediterranean Sea, to the east of Greece, between modern Turkey and Greece.

Areopagus The old aristocratic council of nobles at Athens whose powers were reduced by Pericles in 461 BCE.

Assembly The meeting of all male Athenians over the age of eighteen that was held four times a month.

Council The group of 500 Athenians chosen by lot at village level to prepare business for the Assembly and to put its decisions into operation.

hoplite A heavily armed Greek infantryman who fought in battle.

Isthmus of Corinth The narrow stretch of land connecting mainland Greece to the Peloponnese.

Kerameikos An area just outside the walls of Athens where the dead were buried.

Mediterranean Sea The large continental sea that has its entry at Gibraltar in the west and leads into the Black Sea in the east.

Odeion The covered hall built by Pericles next to the theater for concerts and poetry recitations.

ostracism A meeting at which an Athenian citizen could write down on a piece of pottery the name of a politician who he thought ought to be expelled from the city, a separation that usually lasted ten years.

paidagogos A domestic slave whose main job was to look after the children in a family.

palaestra An open square area surrounded by a colonnade where Athenian citizens would practice sports and relax after running.

Parthenon The most famous temple in Greece built by Pericles and completed in 438 BCE to replace the temple burnt down by the Persians in 480 BCE.

pediment The triangular gable areas at the front and back of a temple, made by the slope of the roof, where decorative sculptures were placed.

Peloponnese The peninsula in southern Greece attached to the mainland of Greece by the Isthmus of Corinth.

Piraeus The port of Athens connected to the main city by walls some six miles long.

Pnyx An open area with a speakers' platform near the Acropolis, where the Athenian Assembly met.

Propylaea The monumental gateway on the Acropolis built by Pericles.

strategos A general at Athens who might be one of ten who were also in charge of administration in and around Athens.

theater An open-air auditorium usually hollowed out from a hillside in a horseshoe shape.

trireme A Greek warship, manned by 170 free citizens, whose main armament was its ram.

American Classical League
Miami University
Oxford, OH 45056
Website: http://www.aclclassics.org
This organization offers job placement assistance, scholarships, workshops, and other learning opportunities for learning about classical Greek and Latin in the US and Canada.

Canadian Museum of History
100 Laurier Street
Gatineau, QC K1A 0M8
Canada
(800) 555-5621
Website: http://www.historymuseum.ca
This museum offers research, activities, school programs, and other opportunities to engage with domestic and ancient history. Additionally, it offers a search engine for its collections at the Canadian Museum of History and the Canadian War Museum.

The Classical Association
University of London
Senate House, Malet Street
Room 323, Third Floor
London WC1E 7HU
United Kingdom
Website: http://www.classicalassociation.org
This organization is dedicated to the development and maintenance of classical studies. It offers publications

and events that are meant to help members and classics enthusiasts to learn about different topics and methods of teaching.

Institute for the Study of the Ancient World
15 East 84th Street
New York, NY 10028
(212) 992-7800
Website: http://isaw.nyu.edu
This organization offers events and exhibitions that allow participants to learn about important questions concerning ancient cultures. Its scholarly community offers opportunities for graduate research and education.

International Plutarch Society
Utah State University
Department of History
0710 Old Main Hill
Logan, UT 84322
Website: http://ips.ploutarchos.org
This organization publishes *Ploutarchos n.s.*, an international scholarly journal consisting of research on the works of Plutarch. Its main goal is to encourage communication between Plutarchan scholars.

Museum of Classical Antiquities
Desmarais Building
55 Laurier Avenue East, 3th Floor

Ottawa, ON
Canada
(613) 562-5800
Website: http://arts.uottawa.ca/cla-srs/en/museum
This museum, founded by the University of Ottawa's Department of Classics, offers workshops, activities, and exercises that are a part of its classics program.

National Junior Classical League
860 NW Washington Boulevard, Suite A
Hamilton, OH 45013
Website: http://www.njcl.org
This student organization serves an international membership by offering conventions, contests, and leadership opportunities that allow young members to engage with and learn about classical antiquity.

Society for Classical Studies
New York University
20 Cooper Square 2nd Floor
New York, NY 10003
(212) 992-7828
Website: https://classicalstudies.org
This society facilitates in the study of Greek and Roman languages and cultural studies by offering fellowships and networking opportunities, and it points users toward job opportunities for professionals.

WEBSITES

Because of the changing nature of internet links, Rosen Publishing has developed an online list of websites related to the subject of this book. This site is updated regularly. Please use this link to access the list:

http://www.rosenlinks.com/LANW/pericles

Allan, Tony, and Sara Maitland. *Ancient Greece and Rome* (World Mythologies). New York, NY: Rosen Publishing, 2012.

Anderson, Marilyn. *Ancient Greece* (Ancient Civilizations). New York, NY: Britannica, 2012.

Everitt, Anthony. *The Rise of Athens: The Story of the World's Greatest Civilization*. New York, NY: Random House, 2016.

Foster, Edith. *Thucydides, Pericles, and Periclean Imperialism*. Cambridge, UK: Cambridge University Press, 2013.

Kuiper, Kathleen. *Ancient Greece* (The Britannica Guide to Ancient Civilizations). New York, NY: Britannica, 2011.

Lanni, Adriaan. *Law and Order in Ancient Athens*. Cambridge, UK: Cambridge University Press, 2016.

Powell, Anton. *Athens and Sparta: Constructing Greek Political and Social History from 478 BC*. 3rd ed. London, UK: Routledge, 2016.

Rankov, Boris (editor). *Trireme Olympias: The Final Report*. Oxford, UK: Oxbow Books, 2012.

Shear, T. Leslie, Jr.. *Trophies of Victory: Public Building in Periklean Athens*. Princeton, NJ: Princeton University Press, 2016.

Taylor, Martha. *Thucydides, Pericles, and the Idea of Athens in the Peloponnesian War*. Cambridge, UK: Cambridge University Press, 2014.

Abbott, Evelyn. *Pericles and the Golden Age of Athens*. London, UK: Forgotten Books, 2016.

Aristophanes (translated by Alan H. Sommerstein). *Lysistrata/The Acharnians/The Clouds*. London, UK: Penguin Books, 1973.

Azoulay, Vincent, Janet Lloyd (translator), Paul Cartledge (foreword). *Pericles of Athens*. Princeton, NJ: Princeton University Press, 2014.

Barrow, Mandy. "Ancient Greece." 2013. http://www.primaryhomeworkhelp.co.uk/greece/food.htm.

Dallas Learning Solutions. "The Meaning of Democracy." Retrieved October 3, 2016. https://dlc.dcccd.edu/usgov1-1/the-meaning-of-democracy.

Gregory, Timothy E. "Geography, Environment, and Archaeology in Greece." Ohio State University. Retrieved October 3, 2016. https://greekarchaeology.osu.edu/arch-edu/archaeology.

Jones, A. H. M. *Athenian Democracy*. Oxford, UK: Blackwell, 1960.

Kagan, Donald. *Pericles of Athens and the Birth of Democracy*. London, UK: Guild, 1990.

Long, Roderick T. "The Athenian Constitution: Government by Jury and Referendum." *Formulations*, Autumn 1996. http://www.freenation.org/a/f41l1.html.

Martin, Thomas. *Pericles: A Biography in Context*. Cambridge, UK: Cambridge University Press, 2016.

Meier, Christian. *Athens: A Portrait of the City in Its Golden Age*. London, UK: John Murray, 1998.

Morris, Ian. "The Growth of Greek Cities in the First Millennium BC." *Princeton/Stanford Working Papers in Classics*. Stanford, CA: Stanford University, December 2005. http://www.princeton.edu/~pswpc/pdfs/morris/120509.pdf.

Morrison, J. S., J. F. Coates, and N. B. Rankov. *The Athenian Trireme*. Cambridge, UK: Cambridge University Press, 2000.

Plutarch (translated by Ian Scott-Kilvert). *The Rise and Fall of Athens*. London, UK: Penguin Books, 1976.

Samons, Loren J., II. *Pericles and the Conquest of History: A Political Biography*. Cambridge, UK: Cambridge University Press, 2016.

Sophocles (translated by Robert Fagles). *The Three Theban Plays*. London, UK: Penguin Books, 1984.

Thompson, Homer A. "Stone, Tile and Timber." *Expedition Magazine* 22.3, Penn Museum, March 1980. http://www.penn.museum/sites/expedition/stone-tile-and-timber.

Thucydides (translated by Rex Warner). *History of the Peloponnesian War*. London, UK: Penguin Books, 1990.

Tracy, Stephen V. *Pericles: A Sourcebook and Reader*. Oakland, CA: University of California Press, 2009.

University of Vermont. "Persian Wars Timeline." Retrieved October 3, 2016. www.uvm.edu/~jbailly/courses/clas21/notes/herodotustimeline.html.

A

Acropolis, 25, 73
  rebuilding of, 53, 56–63, 65
Aegean Sea, 34, 36, 83
Aegina, 50
Agariste, 12
Anaxagoras, 14, 15–17, 19, 21
Antigone, 69
Areopagus, 36–37
Aristophanes, 71–72, 83
Aspasia, 76–77, 95
Assembly, 25, 27–34, 37, 43, 54, 66, 75, 79
Athena, 26, 56, 60–63, 65, 66, 77
Athenian army, makeup and training, 38
Athenian navy, 30, 34, 40–46, 49
Athens
  army, makeup and training, 38
  democracy, 6, 12, 30, 31, 97
  literacy, 13
  navy, 30, 34, 40–46, 49
  slavery, 12–13, 30–33, 43, 58, 79
athletics, importance of, 14
Attica, 29, 33, 61, 65, 68, 88, 93, 94
Azoulay, Vincent, 8

B

Boeotia, 49, 50, 65
building materials, 56–57

C

Callias, 76
Callicrates, 56, 58
Cimon, 23, 34–36, 37, 49
clay/red clay, as building material, 56–57
Cleisthenes, 12
comedies, 71–72
constitutional democracy, 31
Corcyra/Corfu, 84–85
Corinth, 50, 51, 52, 83, 84–85
Council, 28–29, 37
Cyprus, 50

D

Damon, 14, 15, 21
Darius I, 20

democracy, types of, 31
Dionysia, 73
direct democracy, 30, 31
drama, 67–72, 73, 75–76, 79
  comedies, 71–72
  tragedies, 69, 71

E

Egypt, 50
Ephialtes, 36–37, 47
Euboea, 51

F

federal democracy, 31
festivals, 14, 61–63, 72–73, 75, 79
food/diet, 70–71

G

Greco-Persian Wars, 20, 23, 83

H

Herodotus, 7, 8, 21
Homer, 13, 15
hoplites, 38, 39, 40, 51
house construction, 57
Hymettos, 57

I

Ictinus, 56, 58
Ionia, 12, 15, 20, 76

L

Lenaea, 73
Leonidas, 40
limestone, 58
literacy, 13

M

Macedonia, 57
Marathon, Battle of, 20
marble, as building material, 57, 58
Megara, 49, 50, 85, 88
music, belief of moral effect of, 13–14

N

non-constitutional democracy, 31

O

Odeion, 75
ostracism, 33, 37, 49

P

Parnes, Mt., 57
Parthenon, rebuilding of, 56–63, 66
Peloponnesian War, 84–85, 86, 88, 94
Pentelikon, 57
Pericles
  childhood, 10–13
  death, 94–95
  education and teachers, 13–19
  influence on entertainment/theater, 67–76
  legacy/contributions, 95–98
  political life, 23–26, 27–34, 36–37, 43, 47–52, 81–83, 86–94
  rebuilding projects, 53–66
  wife and family, 76, 95
Pericles of Athens, 8
Persians/Persian Empire, 6, 10, 11, 12, 20–21, 23, 26, 34–36, 40, 50, 52, 53, 83, 87
Pheidias, 56, 61, 63, 66
Piraeus, 21, 42, 49, 52, 53
plague, 91–93, 94, 95
Plataea, Battle of, 12
Plutarch, 7, 11, 65, 66, 76, 94, 97
Pnyx, 25, 26, 27, 29
Poseidon, 61, 65
Potidaea, 85
Propylaea, 63

R

representative democracy/republic, 31

S

Salamis, 21
Samos, 82
sandstone, 58
Scythian archers, 27
slaves/slavery, 12–13, 30–33, 43, 58, 79
Sophocles, 67–69
Sparta, 39–40, 50, 51, 52, 55, 72, 80, 83, 84–85, 88, 93, 94, 97
stone, as building material, 56, 57, 58

T

temples, construction of, 57,

58
Thasos, 36
theaters, 19, 73–75, 79
Themistocles, 40
Thermopylae, Pass of, 40
Thrace, 57
Thucydides, 7, 8, 44–46, 83–85, 86, 91–93, 97
tragedies, 69, 71
triremes, 21, 42–43, 88

U

unitary democracy, 31

W

women, role of, 30, 76–80
wood, as building material, 56, 57, 82

X

Xanthippus (father), 12, 21, 23, 33, 76
Xerxes I, 9, 20, 40

Z

Zeus, 60, 61

ABOUT THE AUTHORS

Beatriz Santillian earned her BA in English in 2003 and her PhD in history in 2009. She is a fan of all things to do with ancient history and loves to learn about artifacts from the past. Santillian writes on topics to do with culture, technology, and change, and she also writes software in her spare time. She lives in Rochester, New York, with her daughter.

Hamish Aird is a graduate of Christ Church, Oxford, England, where he read classical languages, history, and philosophy. He served as the sub warden (deputy headmaster) at Radley College, Oxfordshire, England, where he taught Latin and Greek languages and ancient history. He has traveled extensively in the Mediterranean countries and has led groups of teachers on study tours in Greece. He retired in 2016.

PHOTO CREDITS

Cover, p. 3 Gilmanshin/Shutterstock.com; cover (background), p. 84 DEA/Biblioteca Ambrosiana/De Agostini/Getty Images; pp. 6–7 Ken Welsh/Perspectives/Getty Images, pp. 10–11 Ingram Publishing/Thinkstock; p. 16 Heritage Images/Hulton Archive/Getty Images; pp. 18–19 Hulton Archive/Hulton Royals Collection/Getty Images; p. 22 Science Museum/SSPL/Getty Images; pp. 24–25 Philip and Elizabeth De Bay/Corbis Historical/Getty Images; pp. 28–29 Constantinos Iliopoulos/Shutterstock.com; p. 32 Album/Prisma/Superstock; pp. 34–35 Hulton Archive/Getty Images; pp. 40–41 © North Wind Pictures Archives; pp. 44–45 Windmill Books/Universal Images Group/Getty Images; pp. 48–49 Ivan Vdovin/age footstock/SuperStock; pp. 54–55 Kean Collection/Archive Photos/Getty Images; pp. 58–59 Chronicle/Alamy Stock Photo; p. 62 Erich Lessing/Art Resource, NY; p. 64 VWB photos/Moment/Getty Images; pp. 68–69 Robbie Jack/Corbis/Getty Images; pp. 70–71 Stefano Bianchetti/Corbis Historical/Getty Images; p. 73 Private Collection/© Look and Learn/Bridgeman Images; pp. 74–75 Patricia Fenn Gallery/Moment/Getty Images; p. 78 Dorling Kindersley/Thinkstock; p. 82 Lanmas/Alamy Stock Photo; p. 89 Time Life Pictures/The LIFE Picture Collection/Getty Images; pp. 92–93 Pictorial Press Ltd/Alamy Stock Photo; p. 96 Leemage/Corbis Historical/Getty Images; interior pages background images © iStockphoto.com/kikkalek5050 (sky), Triff/Shutterstock.com(map).

Designer: Brian Garvey; Editor: Bernadette Davis; Photo Researcher: Sherri Jackson